THIS FIELD OBSERVATION NOTEBOOK BELONGS TO:

_____

IN THE EVENT THAT THIS NOTEBOOK IS FOUND:

☐ Please return it to me—it has important research notes and stuff!

☐ I mean, not that important, but still, I'd like it back.

☐ Don't read it, though. I put some pretty personal stuff in there, which I
sort of regret doing now. Ha ha, I mean, not like weird stuff! Just, um...
Seriously, please don't read it.

☐ Fine. I don't care. Just burn the stupid thing when you're done.

PLEASE CONTACT ME AT:

_____

_____

_____

REWARD FOR RETURN:

☐ There is a **reward** of **money** if you return it! **$**_____

☐ Doing the right thing should really be reward enough, don't you think?

☐ What kind of person are you?

The Big Dumb Bird Journal

A Field Notebook for Recording Notes, Sketches, and Observations of Birds and their Nonsense

by Matt Kracht

CHRONICLE BOOKS
SAN FRANCISCO

Library of Congress Cataloging-in-Publication Data available.
ISBN 978-1-7972-1628-7

Manufactured in India.

Illustration and design by Matt Kracht.

Chronicle Books LLC
680 Second Street
San Francisco, CA 94107

www.chroniclebooks.com

1 0 9 8 7 6 5 4 3 2

ABOUT THIS BIRD JOURNAL

I'm going to go out on a limb here and assume that you have, at the very least, a basic grasp of what a journal is and how to use one (i.e., you write in it).

This particular notebook is intended for those who wish to observe and document birds and therefore has a number of areas specifically designed for bird-specific information (each heading will be explained further in the next section).

That said, if birds are not your thing, I suppose that this journal could easily be adapted for recording your observations about whatever does interest you—rocks, or pinecones or something. It's up to you, I guess Happy birding or whatever.

RECORDING YOUR OBSERVATIONS

DATE, TIMES & LOCATION

These should be fairly self-explanatory. It can be valuable to note when and where you observed a particular bird or birds; it may help you discern important patterns over time. Also, in my experience, it can help get the type of person who say things like, *"No, no, it couldn't have been a painted bunting. Not in January!"* to shut their self-sure pie hole.

WEATHER

Jotting down the weather conditions at the time of observation maybe of value to bird science, but probably not. Whatever you decide, it will help spark the memories of your glorious experiences watching birds in nature, whether they were during pouring rainstorms or insufferable heat.

NAME OF BIRD

Just put down the name of the bird you see. If you're not sure, put a question mark. Maybe you can fill it in later when you figure it out. Or just make something up. Who's going to know?

NOTES

This is where you can jot down any observations on bird appearance, behavior, or any suspicious activity that you observe.

SKETCHES

Sketch or draw the birds. Alternatively, you could just draw how they make you feel. This can be therapeutic.

REFERENCE

I have included some helpful reference pages in the back of this journal, so refer to them regularly. Or don't. I mean, I did put some real effort into this.

FIELD OBSERVATIONS

DATE _____   LOCATION _____

TIME _____   WEATHER _____

NAME OF BIRD _____

NOTES _____

_____

_____

_____

_____

_____

_____

SKETCHES OF STUPID BIRD YOU SAW

FIELD OBSERVATIONS

DATE ....   LOCATION ....

TIME ....   WEATHER ....

NAME OF BIRD ....

NOTES ....

....

....

....

....

....

....

SKETCHES OF STUPID BIRD YOU SAW

FIELD OBSERVATIONS

DATE _____   LOCATION _____

TIME _____   WEATHER _____

NAME OF BIRD _____

NOTES _____

_____

_____

_____

_____

_____

_____

SKETCHES OF STUPID BIRD YOU SAW

FACT: A hummingbird spends less than one minute of its lifespan reflecting on its own attitude.

FIELD OBSERVATIONS

DATE _____   LOCATION _____

TIME _____   WEATHER _____

NAME OF BIRD _____

NOTES _____

_____

_____

_____

_____

_____

_____

SKETCHES OF STUPID BIRD YOU SAW

FIELD OBSERVATIONS

DATE _____   LOCATION _____

TIME _____   WEATHER _____

NAME OF BIRD _____

NOTES _____

_____

_____

_____

_____

_____

_____

_____

SKETCHES OF STUPID BIRD YOU SAW

FIELD OBSERVATIONS

DATE _____   LOCATION _____

TIME _____   WEATHER _____

NAME OF BIRD _____

NOTES _____

_____

_____

_____

_____

_____

_____

_____

SKETCHES OF STUPID BIRD YOU SAW

FIELD OBSERVATIONS

DATE _____   LOCATION _____

TIME _____   WEATHER _____

NAME OF BIRD _____

NOTES _____

_____

_____

_____

_____

_____

_____

SKETCHES OF STUPID BIRD YOU SAW

FIELD OBSERVATIONS

DATE .... LOCATION ....
TIME .... WEATHER ....

NAME OF BIRD ....

NOTES ....

....

....

....

....

....

....

SKETCHES OF STUPID BIRD YOU SAW

FIELD OBSERVATIONS

DATE _____   LOCATION _____

TIME _____   WEATHER _____

NAME OF BIRD _____

NOTES _____

_____

_____

_____

_____

_____

_____

SKETCHES OF STUPID BIRD YOU SAW

FIELD OBSERVATIONS

DATE .... LOCATION ....

TIME .... WEATHER ....

NAME OF BIRD ....

NOTES ....

....

....

....

....

....

....

SKETCHES OF STUPID BIRD YOU SAW

 **FACT:** Remember, the tiny golden-crowned kinglet is a king only in its own mind.

FIELD OBSERVATIONS

DATE _____   LOCATION _____

TIME _____   WEATHER _____

NAME OF BIRD _____

NOTES _____

_____

_____

_____

_____

_____

_____

SKETCHES OF STUPID BIRD YOU SAW

FIELD OBSERVATIONS

DATE _____   LOCATION _____

TIME _____   WEATHER _____

NAME OF BIRD _____

NOTES _____

_____

_____

_____

_____

_____

_____

SKETCHES OF STUPID BIRD YOU SAW

FIELD OBSERVATIONS

DATE _____   LOCATION _____

TIME _____   WEATHER _____

NAME OF BIRD _____

NOTES _____

_____

_____

_____

_____

_____

_____

SKETCHES OF STUPID BIRD YOU SAW

FIELD OBSERVATIONS

DATE _____   LOCATION _____

TIME _____   WEATHER _____

NAME OF BIRD _____

NOTES _____

_____

_____

_____

_____

_____

_____

SKETCHES OF STUPID BIRD YOU SAW

FIELD OBSERVATIONS

DATE _____   LOCATION _____

TIME _____   WEATHER _____

NAME OF BIRD _____

NOTES _____

_____

_____

_____

_____

_____

_____

SKETCHES OF STUPID BIRD YOU SAW

FIELD OBSERVATIONS

DATE _____   LOCATION _____

TIME _____   WEATHER _____

NAME OF BIRD _____

NOTES _____

_____

_____

_____

_____

_____

_____

_____

SKETCHES OF STUPID BIRD YOU SAW

FACT: If you tell someone you spotted an eagle they will say, "Cool!" But they don't mean it.

FIELD OBSERVATIONS

DATE _____   LOCATION _____

TIME _____   WEATHER _____

NAME OF BIRD _____

NOTES _____

_____

_____

_____

_____

_____

_____

SKETCHES OF STUPID BIRD YOU SAW

FIELD OBSERVATIONS

DATE _____   LOCATION _____

TIME _____   WEATHER _____

NAME OF BIRD _____

NOTES _____

_____

_____

_____

_____

_____

_____

SKETCHES OF STUPID BIRD YOU SAW

FIELD OBSERVATIONS

DATE ....

LOCATION ....

TIME ....

WEATHER ....

NAME OF BIRD ....

NOTES ....

....

....

....

....

....

....

....

SKETCHES OF STUPID BIRD YOU SAW

FACT: The Kentucky warbler's bright plumage and cheerful song mask its deep insecurities.

FIELD OBSERVATIONS

DATE _____   LOCATION _____

TIME _____   WEATHER _____

NAME OF BIRD _____

NOTES _____

_____

_____

_____

_____

_____

_____

SKETCHES OF STUPID BIRD YOU SAW

FIELD OBSERVATIONS

DATE _____   LOCATION _____

TIME _____   WEATHER _____

NAME OF BIRD _____

NOTES _____

_____

_____

_____

_____

_____

_____

SKETCHES OF STUPID BIRD YOU SAW

FIELD OBSERVATIONS

DATE _____   LOCATION _____

TIME _____   WEATHER _____

NAME OF BIRD _____

NOTES _____

_____

_____

_____

_____

_____

_____

_____

SKETCHES OF STUPID BIRD YOU SAW

FIELD OBSERVATIONS

DATE _____   LOCATION _____

TIME _____   WEATHER _____

NAME OF BIRD _____

NOTES _____

_____

_____

_____

_____

_____

_____

SKETCHES OF STUPID BIRD YOU SAW

FIELD OBSERVATIONS

DATE _____   LOCATION _____

TIME _____   WEATHER _____

NAME OF BIRD _____

NOTES _____

_____

_____

_____

_____

_____

_____

SKETCHES OF STUPID BIRD YOU SAW

FIELD OBSERVATIONS

DATE _____   LOCATION _____

TIME _____   WEATHER _____

NAME OF BIRD _____

NOTES _____

_____

_____

_____

_____

_____

_____

SKETCHES OF STUPID BIRD YOU SAW

FIELD OBSERVATIONS

DATE .... LOCATION ....

TIME .... WEATHER ....

NAME OF BIRD ....

NOTES ....

....

....

....

....

....

....

....

SKETCHES OF STUPID BIRD YOU SAW

FACT: Barn swallows can be found almost everywhere in the world, unfortunately.

FIELD OBSERVATIONS

DATE _____   LOCATION _____

TIME _____   WEATHER _____

NAME OF BIRD _____

NOTES _____

_____

_____

_____

_____

_____

_____

SKETCHES OF STUPID BIRD YOU SAW

FIELD OBSERVATIONS

DATE _____   LOCATION _____

TIME _____   WEATHER _____

NAME OF BIRD _____

NOTES _____

_____

_____

_____

_____

_____

_____

_____

SKETCHES OF STUPID BIRD YOU SAW

FIELD OBSERVATIONS

DATE _____   LOCATION _____

TIME _____   WEATHER _____

NAME OF BIRD _____

NOTES _____

_____

_____

_____

_____

_____

_____

SKETCHES OF STUPID BIRD YOU SAW

FIELD OBSERVATIONS

DATE _____   LOCATION _____

TIME _____   WEATHER _____

NAME OF BIRD _____

NOTES _____

_____

_____

_____

_____

_____

_____

_____

SKETCHES OF STUPID BIRD YOU SAW

FIELD OBSERVATIONS

DATE _____   LOCATION _____

TIME _____   WEATHER _____

NAME OF BIRD _____

NOTES _____

_____

_____

_____

_____

_____

_____

SKETCHES OF STUPID BIRD YOU SAW

FIELD OBSERVATIONS

DATE _____ LOCATION _____

TIME _____ WEATHER _____

NAME OF BIRD _____

NOTES _____

_____

_____

_____

_____

_____

_____

_____

SKETCHES OF STUPID BIRD YOU SAW

 **FACT:** Pigeons are so common that seeing one is not even considered birdwatching.

FIELD OBSERVATIONS

DATE _____   LOCATION _____
TIME _____   WEATHER _____

NAME OF BIRD _____

NOTES _____

_____

_____

_____

_____

_____

_____

SKETCHES OF STUPID BIRD YOU SAW

FIELD OBSERVATIONS

DATE _____   LOCATION _____

TIME _____   WEATHER _____

NAME OF BIRD _____

NOTES _____

_____

_____

_____

_____

_____

_____

_____

SKETCHES OF STUPID BIRD YOU SAW

FIELD OBSERVATIONS

DATE _____   LOCATION _____

TIME _____   WEATHER _____

NAME OF BIRD _____

NOTES _____

_____

_____

_____

_____

_____

_____

SKETCHES OF STUPID BIRD YOU SAW

FACT: Woodpeckers could quit all that fucking drumming once in a while.

FIELD OBSERVATIONS

DATE _____ LOCATION _____

TIME _____ WEATHER _____

NAME OF BIRD _____

NOTES _____

_____

_____

_____

_____

_____

_____

SKETCHES OF STUPID BIRD YOU SAW

FIELD OBSERVATIONS

DATE _____   LOCATION _____

TIME _____   WEATHER _____

NAME OF BIRD _____

NOTES _____

_____

_____

_____

_____

_____

_____

SKETCHES OF STUPID BIRD YOU SAW

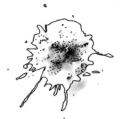

FIELD OBSERVATIONS

DATE _____   LOCATION _____

TIME _____   WEATHER _____

NAME OF BIRD _____

NOTES _____

_____

_____

_____

_____

_____

_____

SKETCHES OF STUPID BIRD YOU SAW

FIELD OBSERVATIONS

DATE _____   LOCATION _____

TIME _____   WEATHER _____

NAME OF BIRD _____

NOTES _____

_____

_____

_____

_____

_____

_____

SKETCHES OF STUPID BIRD YOU SAW

FIELD OBSERVATIONS

DATE ....   LOCATION ....

TIME ....   WEATHER ....

NAME OF BIRD ....

NOTES ....

....

....

....

....

....

....

....

SKETCHES OF STUPID BIRD YOU SAW

FIELD OBSERVATIONS

DATE _____   LOCATION _____

TIME _____   WEATHER _____

NAME OF BIRD _____

NOTES _____

_____

_____

_____

_____

_____

_____

SKETCHES OF STUPID BIRD YOU SAW

FIELD OBSERVATIONS

DATE _____   LOCATION _____

TIME _____   WEATHER _____

NAME OF BIRD _____

NOTES _____

_____

_____

_____

_____

_____

_____

SKETCHES OF STUPID BIRD YOU SAW

FACT: The red-breasted merganser has the worst haircut of all the ducks.

FIELD OBSERVATIONS

DATE ....   LOCATION ....

TIME ....   WEATHER ....

NAME OF BIRD ....

NOTES ....

....

....

....

....

....

....

....

SKETCHES OF STUPID BIRD YOU SAW

FIELD OBSERVATIONS

DATE _____   LOCATION _____

TIME _____   WEATHER _____

NAME OF BIRD _____

NOTES _____

_____

_____

_____

_____

_____

_____

_____

SKETCHES OF STUPID BIRD YOU SAW

FIELD OBSERVATIONS

DATE _____   LOCATION _____

TIME _____   WEATHER _____

NAME OF BIRD _____

NOTES _____

_____

_____

_____

_____

_____

_____

SKETCHES OF STUPID BIRD YOU SAW

FIELD OBSERVATIONS

DATE _____   LOCATION _____

TIME _____   WEATHER _____

NAME OF BIRD _____

NOTES _____

_____

_____

_____

_____

_____

_____

_____

SKETCHES OF STUPID BIRD YOU SAW

 **FACT:** Cranes—you really don't hear much about them these days, do you?

FIELD OBSERVATIONS

DATE _____   LOCATION _____

TIME _____   WEATHER _____

NAME OF BIRD _____

NOTES _____

_____

_____

_____

_____

_____

_____

SKETCHES OF STUPID BIRD YOU SAW

FIELD OBSERVATIONS

DATE ....

LOCATION ....

TIME ....

WEATHER ....

NAME OF BIRD ....

NOTES ....

....

....

....

....

....

....

....

SKETCHES OF STUPID BIRD YOU SAW

FIELD OBSERVATIONS

DATE _____   LOCATION _____

TIME _____   WEATHER _____

NAME OF BIRD _____

NOTES _____

_____

_____

_____

_____

_____

_____

_____

SKETCHES OF STUPID BIRD YOU SAW

FACT: A hummingbird can ignore the feelings of others eighty times per second!

FIELD OBSERVATIONS

DATE _____ LOCATION _____

TIME _____ WEATHER _____

NAME OF BIRD _____

NOTES _____

_____

_____

_____

_____

_____

_____

SKETCHES OF STUPID BIRD YOU SAW

FIELD OBSERVATIONS

DATE _____   LOCATION _____

TIME _____   WEATHER _____

NAME OF BIRD _____

NOTES _____

_____

_____

_____

_____

_____

_____

SKETCHES OF STUPID BIRD YOU SAW

FIELD OBSERVATIONS

DATE _____   LOCATION _____

TIME _____   WEATHER _____

NAME OF BIRD _____

NOTES _____

_____

_____

_____

_____

_____

_____

_____

SKETCHES OF STUPID BIRD YOU SAW

FIELD OBSERVATIONS

DATE _____   LOCATION _____

TIME _____   WEATHER _____

NAME OF BIRD _____

NOTES _____

_____

_____

_____

_____

_____

_____

SKETCHES OF STUPID BIRD YOU SAW

FIELD OBSERVATIONS

DATE .... LOCATION ....

TIME .... WEATHER ....

NAME OF BIRD ....

NOTES ....

....

....

....

....

....

....

SKETCHES OF STUPID BIRD YOU SAW

FIELD OBSERVATIONS

DATE _____   LOCATION _____

TIME _____   WEATHER _____

NAME OF BIRD _____

NOTES _____

_____

_____

_____

_____

_____

_____

SKETCHES OF STUPID BIRD YOU SAW

FIELD OBSERVATIONS

DATE _____ LOCATION _____

TIME _____ WEATHER _____

NAME OF BIRD _____

NOTES _____

_____

_____

_____

_____

_____

_____

SKETCHES OF STUPID BIRD YOU SAW

FACT: Crows actually feel no remorse for stealing.

FIELD OBSERVATIONS

DATE _____   LOCATION _____

TIME _____   WEATHER _____

NAME OF BIRD _____

NOTES _____

_____

_____

_____

_____

_____

_____

SKETCHES OF STUPID BIRD YOU SAW

FIELD OBSERVATIONS

DATE _____   LOCATION _____

TIME _____   WEATHER _____

NAME OF BIRD _____

NOTES _____

_____

_____

_____

_____

_____

_____

_____

SKETCHES OF STUPID BIRD YOU SAW

FIELD OBSERVATIONS

DATE _____   LOCATION _____

TIME _____   WEATHER _____

NAME OF BIRD _____

NOTES _____

_____

_____

_____

_____

_____

_____

_____

SKETCHES OF STUPID BIRD YOU SAW

FIELD OBSERVATIONS

DATE _____   LOCATION _____

TIME _____   WEATHER _____

NAME OF BIRD _____

NOTES _____

_____

_____

_____

_____

_____

_____

_____

SKETCHES OF STUPID BIRD YOU SAW

FIELD OBSERVATIONS

DATE _____   LOCATION _____

TIME _____   WEATHER _____

NAME OF BIRD _____

NOTES _____

_____

_____

_____

_____

_____

_____

SKETCHES OF STUPID BIRD YOU SAW

FIELD OBSERVATIONS

DATE _____   LOCATION _____

TIME _____   WEATHER _____

NAME OF BIRD _____

NOTES _____

_____

_____

_____

_____

_____

_____

SKETCHES OF STUPID BIRD YOU SAW

 **FACT:** Ducks spend a lot of time floating around when they could be doing something.

FIELD OBSERVATIONS

DATE _____   LOCATION _____

TIME _____   WEATHER _____

NAME OF BIRD _____

NOTES _____

_____

_____

_____

_____

_____

_____

SKETCHES OF STUPID BIRD YOU SAW

FIELD OBSERVATIONS

DATE ....   LOCATION ....

TIME ....   WEATHER ....

NAME OF BIRD ....

NOTES ....

....

....

....

....

....

....

SKETCHES OF STUPID BIRD YOU SAW

FIELD OBSERVATIONS

DATE _____   LOCATION _____

TIME _____   WEATHER _____

NAME OF BIRD _____

NOTES _____

_____

_____

_____

_____

_____

_____

SKETCHES OF STUPID BIRD YOU SAW

 **FACT:** The ruby-crowned kinglet resembles a cocktail olive but does not taste like one.

FIELD OBSERVATIONS

DATE _____   LOCATION _____

TIME _____   WEATHER _____

NAME OF BIRD _____

NOTES _____

_____

_____

_____

_____

_____

_____

SKETCHES OF STUPID BIRD YOU SAW

FIELD OBSERVATIONS

DATE _____   LOCATION _____

TIME _____   WEATHER _____

NAME OF BIRD _____

NOTES _____

_____

_____

_____

_____

_____

_____

SKETCHES OF STUPID BIRD YOU SAW

FIELD OBSERVATIONS

DATE ....

TIME ....

LOCATION ....

WEATHER ....

NAME OF BIRD ....

NOTES ....

....

....

....

....

....

....

....

SKETCHES OF STUPID BIRD YOU SAW

FIELD OBSERVATIONS

DATE _____   LOCATION _____

TIME _____   WEATHER _____

NAME OF BIRD _____

NOTES _____

_____

_____

_____

_____

_____

_____

SKETCHES OF STUPID BIRD YOU SAW

FIELD OBSERVATIONS

DATE _____   LOCATION _____

TIME _____   WEATHER _____

NAME OF BIRD _____

NOTES _____

_____

_____

_____

_____

_____

_____

_____

SKETCHES OF STUPID BIRD YOU SAW

FIELD OBSERVATIONS

DATE _____   LOCATION _____

TIME _____   WEATHER _____

NAME OF BIRD _____

NOTES _____

_____

_____

_____

_____

_____

_____

SKETCHES OF STUPID BIRD YOU SAW

FIELD OBSERVATIONS

DATE _____   LOCATION _____

TIME _____   WEATHER _____

NAME OF BIRD _____

NOTES _____

_____

_____

_____

_____

_____

_____

SKETCHES OF STUPID BIRD YOU SAW

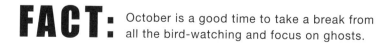

FACT: October is a good time to take a break from all the bird-watching and focus on ghosts.

FIELD OBSERVATIONS

DATE _____   LOCATION _____

TIME _____   WEATHER _____

NAME OF BIRD _____

NOTES _____

_____

_____

_____

_____

_____

_____

_____

SKETCHES OF STUPID BIRD YOU SAW

FIELD OBSERVATIONS

DATE _____   LOCATION _____

TIME _____   WEATHER _____

NAME OF BIRD _____

NOTES _____

_____

_____

_____

_____

_____

_____

_____

SKETCHES OF STUPID BIRD YOU SAW

FIELD OBSERVATIONS

DATE _____   LOCATION _____

TIME _____   WEATHER _____

NAME OF BIRD _____

NOTES _____

_____

_____

_____

_____

_____

_____

_____

SKETCHES OF STUPID BIRD YOU SAW

FIELD OBSERVATIONS

DATE _____   LOCATION _____

TIME _____   WEATHER _____

NAME OF BIRD _____

NOTES _____

_____

_____

_____

_____

_____

_____

SKETCHES OF STUPID BIRD YOU SAW

FIELD OBSERVATIONS

DATE _____   LOCATION _____

TIME _____   WEATHER _____

NAME OF BIRD _____

NOTES _____

_____

_____

_____

_____

_____

_____

_____

SKETCHES OF STUPID BIRD YOU SAW

FIELD OBSERVATIONS

DATE _____   LOCATION _____

TIME _____   WEATHER _____

NAME OF BIRD _____

NOTES _____

_____

_____

_____

_____

_____

_____

SKETCHES OF STUPID BIRD YOU SAW

FACT: Some gulls' eyes change color as they age, but their behavior remains immature.

FIELD OBSERVATIONS

DATE _____   LOCATION _____

TIME _____   WEATHER _____

NAME OF BIRD _____

NOTES _____

_____

_____

_____

_____

_____

_____

SKETCHES OF STUPID BIRD YOU SAW

FIELD OBSERVATIONS

DATE ....   LOCATION ....

TIME ....   WEATHER ....

NAME OF BIRD ....

NOTES ....

....

....

....

....

....

....

....

SKETCHES OF STUPID BIRD YOU SAW

FIELD OBSERVATIONS

DATE _____   LOCATION _____

TIME _____   WEATHER _____

NAME OF BIRD _____

NOTES _____

_____

_____

_____

_____

_____

_____

SKETCHES OF STUPID BIRD YOU SAW

FACT: If a jay scolds you it is probably more about their own issues than it is about you.

FIELD OBSERVATIONS

DATE .... LOCATION ....

TIME .... WEATHER ....

NAME OF BIRD ....

NOTES ....

....

....

....

....

....

....

....

SKETCHES OF STUPID BIRD YOU SAW

FIELD OBSERVATIONS

DATE _____   LOCATION _____

TIME _____   WEATHER _____

NAME OF BIRD _____

NOTES _____

_____

_____

_____

_____

_____

_____

SKETCHES OF STUPID BIRD YOU SAW

FIELD OBSERVATIONS

DATE _____   LOCATION _____

TIME _____   WEATHER _____

NAME OF BIRD _____

NOTES _____

_____

_____

_____

_____

_____

_____

_____

SKETCHES OF STUPID BIRD YOU SAW

FIELD OBSERVATIONS

DATE _____   LOCATION _____

TIME _____   WEATHER _____

NAME OF BIRD _____

NOTES _____

_____

_____

_____

_____

_____

_____

SKETCHES OF STUPID BIRD YOU SAW

FIELD OBSERVATIONS

DATE _____   LOCATION _____

TIME _____   WEATHER _____

NAME OF BIRD _____

NOTES _____

_____

_____

_____

_____

_____

_____

SKETCHES OF STUPID BIRD YOU SAW

FIELD OBSERVATIONS

DATE _____   LOCATION _____

TIME _____   WEATHER _____

NAME OF BIRD _____

NOTES _____

_____

_____

_____

_____

_____

_____

SKETCHES OF STUPID BIRD YOU SAW

FIELD OBSERVATIONS

DATE _____   LOCATION _____

TIME _____   WEATHER _____

NAME OF BIRD _____

NOTES _____

_____

_____

_____

_____

_____

_____

SKETCHES OF STUPID BIRD YOU SAW

FACT: Wilson's warbler is the yellow one that looks like it has a cheap, black toupee.

FIELD OBSERVATIONS

DATE _____   LOCATION _____

TIME _____   WEATHER _____

NAME OF BIRD _____

NOTES _____

_____

_____

_____

_____

_____

_____

SKETCHES OF STUPID BIRD YOU SAW

FIELD OBSERVATIONS

DATE ....   LOCATION ....

TIME ....   WEATHER ....

NAME OF BIRD ....

NOTES ....

....

....

....

....

....

....

....

SKETCHES OF STUPID BIRD YOU SAW

FIELD OBSERVATIONS

DATE _____   LOCATION _____

TIME _____   WEATHER _____

NAME OF BIRD _____

NOTES _____

_____

_____

_____

_____

_____

_____

_____

SKETCHES OF STUPID BIRD YOU SAW

FIELD OBSERVATIONS

DATE ....   LOCATION ....

TIME ....   WEATHER ....

NAME OF BIRD ....

NOTES ....

....

....

....

....

....

....

SKETCHES OF STUPID BIRD YOU SAW

FACT: Cranes and herons: do we really need both?

FIELD OBSERVATIONS

DATE _____   LOCATION _____

TIME _____   WEATHER _____

NAME OF BIRD _____

NOTES _____

_____

_____

_____

_____

_____

_____

_____

SKETCHES OF STUPID BIRD YOU SAW

FIELD OBSERVATIONS

DATE _____   LOCATION _____

TIME _____   WEATHER _____

NAME OF BIRD _____

NOTES _____

_____

_____

_____

_____

_____

_____

_____

SKETCHES OF STUPID BIRD YOU SAW

FIELD OBSERVATIONS

DATE _____   LOCATION _____

TIME _____   WEATHER _____

NAME OF BIRD _____

NOTES _____

_____

_____

_____

_____

_____

_____

_____

SKETCHES OF STUPID BIRD YOU SAW

FIELD OBSERVATIONS

DATE _____   LOCATION _____

TIME _____   WEATHER _____

NAME OF BIRD _____

NOTES _____

_____

_____

_____

_____

_____

_____

SKETCHES OF STUPID BIRD YOU SAW

FIELD OBSERVATIONS

DATE _____ LOCATION _____

TIME _____ WEATHER _____

NAME OF BIRD _____

NOTES _____

_____

_____

_____

_____

_____

_____

_____

SKETCHES OF STUPID BIRD YOU SAW

FACT: Typically, in a flock of geese, none of them knows what they are honking about.

FIELD OBSERVATIONS

DATE _____   LOCATION _____

TIME _____   WEATHER _____

NAME OF BIRD _____

NOTES _____

_____

_____

_____

_____

_____

_____

SKETCHES OF STUPID BIRD YOU SAW

FIELD OBSERVATIONS

DATE _____   LOCATION _____

TIME _____   WEATHER _____

NAME OF BIRD _____

NOTES _____

_____

_____

_____

_____

_____

_____

SKETCHES OF STUPID BIRD YOU SAW

FIELD OBSERVATIONS

DATE _____   LOCATION _____

TIME _____   WEATHER _____

NAME OF BIRD _____

NOTES _____

_____

_____

_____

_____

_____

_____

SKETCHES OF STUPID BIRD YOU SAW

FIELD OBSERVATIONS

DATE _____   LOCATION _____

TIME _____   WEATHER _____

NAME OF BIRD _____

NOTES _____

_____

_____

_____

_____

_____

_____

SKETCHES OF STUPID BIRD YOU SAW

FIELD OBSERVATIONS

DATE .... LOCATION ....

TIME .... WEATHER ....

NAME OF BIRD ....

NOTES ....

....

....

....

....

....

....

....

SKETCHES OF STUPID BIRD YOU SAW

FIELD OBSERVATIONS

DATE _____   LOCATION _____

TIME _____   WEATHER _____

NAME OF BIRD _____

NOTES _____

_____

_____

_____

_____

_____

_____

_____

SKETCHES OF STUPID BIRD YOU SAW

FIELD OBSERVATIONS

DATE ....   LOCATION ....

TIME ....   WEATHER ....

NAME OF BIRD ....

NOTES ....

....

....

....

....

....

....

SKETCHES OF STUPID BIRD YOU SAW

FACT: The higher the altitude, the poorer the attitude.

FIELD OBSERVATIONS

DATE .... LOCATION ....

TIME .... WEATHER ....

NAME OF BIRD ....

NOTES ....

....

....

....

....

....

....

....

SKETCHES OF STUPID BIRD YOU SAW

FIELD OBSERVATIONS

DATE _____   LOCATION _____

TIME _____   WEATHER _____

NAME OF BIRD _____

NOTES _____

_____

_____

_____

_____

_____

_____

SKETCHES OF STUPID BIRD YOU SAW

FIELD OBSERVATIONS

DATE _____   LOCATION _____

TIME _____   WEATHER _____

NAME OF BIRD _____

NOTES _____

_____

_____

_____

_____

_____

_____

SKETCHES OF STUPID BIRD YOU SAW

FIELD OBSERVATIONS

DATE ....
LOCATION ....

TIME ....
WEATHER ....

NAME OF BIRD ....

NOTES ....

....

....

....

....

....

....

SKETCHES OF STUPID BIRD YOU SAW

FIELD OBSERVATIONS

DATE _____   LOCATION _____

TIME _____   WEATHER _____

NAME OF BIRD _____

NOTES _____

_____

_____

_____

_____

_____

_____

_____

SKETCHES OF STUPID BIRD YOU SAW

FIELD OBSERVATIONS

DATE _____   LOCATION _____

TIME _____   WEATHER _____

NAME OF BIRD _____

NOTES _____

_____

_____

_____

_____

_____

_____

SKETCHES OF STUPID BIRD YOU SAW

FACT: There are more than fifty species of seagull, which is way more than we need.

FIELD OBSERVATIONS

DATE _____   LOCATION _____

TIME _____   WEATHER _____

NAME OF BIRD _____

NOTES _____

_____

_____

_____

_____

_____

_____

SKETCHES OF STUPID BIRD YOU SAW

FIELD OBSERVATIONS

DATE _____   LOCATION _____

TIME _____   WEATHER _____

NAME OF BIRD _____

NOTES _____

_____

_____

_____

_____

_____

_____

SKETCHES OF STUPID BIRD YOU SAW

FIELD OBSERVATIONS

DATE _____   LOCATION _____

TIME _____   WEATHER _____

NAME OF BIRD _____

NOTES _____

_____

_____

_____

_____

_____

_____

SKETCHES OF STUPID BIRD YOU SAW

FACT: You should never feed bread to ducks because they do not deserve it.

FIELD OBSERVATIONS

DATE _____   LOCATION _____

TIME _____   WEATHER _____

NAME OF BIRD _____

NOTES _____

_____

_____

_____

_____

_____

_____

SKETCHES OF STUPID BIRD YOU SAW

FIELD OBSERVATIONS

DATE _____   LOCATION _____

TIME _____   WEATHER _____

NAME OF BIRD _____

NOTES _____

_____

_____

_____

_____

_____

_____

SKETCHES OF STUPID BIRD YOU SAW

FIELD OBSERVATIONS

DATE _____   LOCATION _____

TIME _____   WEATHER _____

NAME OF BIRD _____

NOTES _____

_____

_____

_____

_____

_____

_____

_____

SKETCHES OF STUPID BIRD YOU SAW

FIELD OBSERVATIONS

DATE _____   LOCATION _____

TIME _____   WEATHER _____

NAME OF BIRD _____

NOTES _____

_____

_____

_____

_____

_____

_____

_____

SKETCHES OF STUPID BIRD YOU SAW

FIELD OBSERVATIONS

DATE _____   LOCATION _____

TIME _____   WEATHER _____

NAME OF BIRD _____

NOTES _____

_____

_____

_____

_____

_____

_____

_____

SKETCHES OF STUPID BIRD YOU SAW

 **FACT:** "A bird in the hand is worth two in the bush" is wrong if you value good hand hygiene.

FIELD OBSERVATIONS

DATE _____   LOCATION _____

TIME _____   WEATHER _____

NAME OF BIRD _____

NOTES _____

_____

_____

_____

_____

_____

_____

SKETCHES OF STUPID BIRD YOU SAW

FIELD OBSERVATIONS

DATE _____   LOCATION _____

TIME _____   WEATHER _____

NAME OF BIRD _____

NOTES _____

_____

_____

_____

_____

_____

_____

_____

SKETCHES OF STUPID BIRD YOU SAW

FIELD OBSERVATIONS

DATE _____   LOCATION _____

TIME _____   WEATHER _____

NAME OF BIRD _____

NOTES _____

_____

_____

_____

_____

_____

_____

_____

SKETCHES OF STUPID BIRD YOU SAW

FIELD OBSERVATIONS

DATE _____   LOCATION _____

TIME _____   WEATHER _____

NAME OF BIRD _____

NOTES _____

_____

_____

_____

_____

_____

_____

_____

SKETCHES OF STUPID BIRD YOU SAW

FIELD OBSERVATIONS

DATE _____   LOCATION _____

TIME _____   WEATHER _____

NAME OF BIRD _____

NOTES _____

_____

_____

_____

_____

_____

_____

SKETCHES OF STUPID BIRD YOU SAW

FIELD OBSERVATIONS

DATE _____   LOCATION _____

TIME _____   WEATHER _____

NAME OF BIRD _____

NOTES _____

_____

_____

_____

_____

_____

_____

_____

SKETCHES OF STUPID BIRD YOU SAW

FACT: Red-tailed hawks sometimes hunt pigeons, which is a win for everyone.

FIELD OBSERVATIONS

DATE _____   LOCATION _____

TIME _____   WEATHER _____

NAME OF BIRD _____

NOTES _____

_____

_____

_____

_____

_____

_____

_____

SKETCHES OF STUPID BIRD YOU SAW

FIELD OBSERVATIONS

DATE _____   LOCATION _____

TIME _____   WEATHER _____

NAME OF BIRD _____

NOTES _____

_____

_____

_____

_____

_____

_____

_____

SKETCHES OF STUPID BIRD YOU SAW

FIELD OBSERVATIONS

DATE _____ LOCATION _____

TIME _____ WEATHER _____

NAME OF BIRD _____

NOTES _____

_____

_____

_____

_____

_____

_____

SKETCHES OF STUPID BIRD YOU SAW

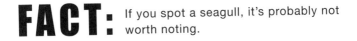

FACT: If you spot a seagull, it's probably not worth noting.

FIELD OBSERVATIONS

DATE _____   LOCATION _____

TIME _____   WEATHER _____

NAME OF BIRD _____

NOTES _____

_____

_____

_____

_____

_____

_____

SKETCHES OF STUPID BIRD YOU SAW

FIELD OBSERVATIONS

DATE _____   LOCATION _____

TIME _____   WEATHER _____

NAME OF BIRD _____

NOTES _____

_____

_____

_____

_____

_____

_____

SKETCHES OF STUPID BIRD YOU SAW

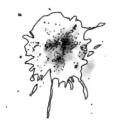

FIELD OBSERVATIONS

DATE _____   LOCATION _____

TIME _____   WEATHER _____

NAME OF BIRD _____

NOTES _____

_____

_____

_____

_____

_____

_____

SKETCHES OF STUPID BIRD YOU SAW

FIELD OBSERVATIONS

DATE _____   LOCATION _____

TIME _____   WEATHER _____

NAME OF BIRD _____

NOTES _____

_____

_____

_____

_____

_____

_____

SKETCHES OF STUPID BIRD YOU SAW

FIELD OBSERVATIONS

DATE _____   LOCATION _____

TIME _____   WEATHER _____

NAME OF BIRD _____

NOTES _____

_____

_____

_____

_____

_____

_____

_____

SKETCHES OF STUPID BIRD YOU SAW

FIELD OBSERVATIONS

DATE _____   LOCATION _____

TIME _____   WEATHER _____

NAME OF BIRD _____

NOTES _____

_____

_____

_____

_____

_____

_____

SKETCHES OF STUPID BIRD YOU SAW

FIELD OBSERVATIONS

DATE _____   LOCATION _____

TIME _____   WEATHER _____

NAME OF BIRD _____

NOTES _____

_____

_____

_____

_____

_____

_____

_____

SKETCHES OF STUPID BIRD YOU SAW

FACT: House sparrows are easy to find, but hard to find interesting.

FIELD OBSERVATIONS

DATE _____   LOCATION _____

TIME _____   WEATHER _____

NAME OF BIRD _____

NOTES _____

_____

_____

_____

_____

_____

_____

SKETCHES OF STUPID BIRD YOU SAW

FIELD OBSERVATIONS

DATE _____   LOCATION _____

TIME _____   WEATHER _____

NAME OF BIRD _____

NOTES _____

_____

_____

_____

_____

_____

_____

_____

SKETCHES OF STUPID BIRD YOU SAW

FIELD OBSERVATIONS

DATE _____   LOCATION _____

TIME _____   WEATHER _____

NAME OF BIRD _____

NOTES _____

_____

_____

_____

_____

_____

_____

SKETCHES OF STUPID BIRD YOU SAW

FIELD OBSERVATIONS

DATE _____   LOCATION _____

TIME _____   WEATHER _____

NAME OF BIRD _____

NOTES _____

_____

_____

_____

_____

_____

_____

SKETCHES OF STUPID BIRD YOU SAW

 **FACT:** Some experts believe that the California quail's distinctive head plume looks stupid.

FIELD OBSERVATIONS

DATE _____ LOCATION _____

TIME _____ WEATHER _____

NAME OF BIRD _____

NOTES _____

_____

_____

_____

_____

_____

_____

SKETCHES OF STUPID BIRD YOU SAW

FIELD OBSERVATIONS

DATE .... LOCATION ....

TIME .... WEATHER ....

NAME OF BIRD ....

NOTES ....

....

....

....

....

....

....

SKETCHES OF STUPID BIRD YOU SAW

FIELD OBSERVATIONS

DATE _____   LOCATION _____

TIME _____   WEATHER _____

NAME OF BIRD _____

NOTES _____

_____

_____

_____

_____

_____

_____

SKETCHES OF STUPID BIRD YOU SAW

FIELD OBSERVATIONS

DATE _____   LOCATION _____

TIME _____   WEATHER _____

NAME OF BIRD _____

NOTES _____

_____

_____

_____

_____

_____

_____

SKETCHES OF STUPID BIRD YOU SAW

FIELD OBSERVATIONS

DATE _____   LOCATION _____

TIME _____   WEATHER _____

NAME OF BIRD _____

NOTES _____

_____

_____

_____

_____

_____

_____

_____

SKETCHES OF STUPID BIRD YOU SAW

FACT: If you spot a house sparrow, don't bother describing it because no one cares.

FIELD OBSERVATIONS

DATE ....   LOCATION ....

TIME ....   WEATHER ....

NAME OF BIRD ....

NOTES ....

....

....

....

....

....

....

SKETCHES OF STUPID BIRD YOU SAW

FIELD OBSERVATIONS

DATE _____   LOCATION _____

TIME _____   WEATHER _____

NAME OF BIRD _____

NOTES _____

_____

_____

_____

_____

_____

_____

SKETCHES OF STUPID BIRD YOU SAW

FIELD OBSERVATIONS

DATE _____   LOCATION _____

TIME _____   WEATHER _____

NAME OF BIRD _____

NOTES _____

_____

_____

_____

_____

_____

_____

_____

SKETCHES OF STUPID BIRD YOU SAW

FIELD OBSERVATIONS

DATE .... LOCATION ....

TIME .... WEATHER ....

NAME OF BIRD ....

NOTES ....

....

....

....

....

....

....

SKETCHES OF STUPID BIRD YOU SAW

FIELD OBSERVATIONS

DATE .... LOCATION ....

TIME .... WEATHER ....

NAME OF BIRD ....

NOTES ....

....

....

....

....

....

....

....

SKETCHES OF STUPID BIRD YOU SAW

FACT: Goldeneye are actually just ducks with large, poorly shaped heads.

FIELD OBSERVATIONS

DATE _____   LOCATION _____

TIME _____   WEATHER _____

NAME OF BIRD _____

NOTES _____

_____

_____

_____

_____

_____

_____

_____

SKETCHES OF STUPID BIRD YOU SAW

FIELD OBSERVATIONS

DATE _____   LOCATION _____

TIME _____   WEATHER _____

NAME OF BIRD _____

NOTES _____

_____

_____

_____

_____

_____

_____

_____

SKETCHES OF STUPID BIRD YOU SAW

FIELD OBSERVATIONS

DATE _____   LOCATION _____

TIME _____   WEATHER _____

NAME OF BIRD _____

NOTES _____

_____

_____

_____

_____

_____

_____

SKETCHES OF STUPID BIRD YOU SAW

FIELD OBSERVATIONS

DATE _____ LOCATION _____

TIME _____ WEATHER _____

NAME OF BIRD _____

NOTES _____

_____

_____

_____

_____

_____

_____

_____

SKETCHES OF STUPID BIRD YOU SAW

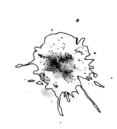

REFERENCE SECTION

Here I have included a selection of reference pages, some practical bird-journaling tips, and space for additional notes, as if anyone cares.

REFERENCE

Birds come in six main shapes. While there are many varia-
tions of each, nature has generally shaped them according
to the type of bird that they are deep down.

THE SIX MAIN
BIRD SHAPES

BASIC

LUMP

ShitSack

FLOATERS

WEIRD LegS

Murder

PARTS of A BIRD

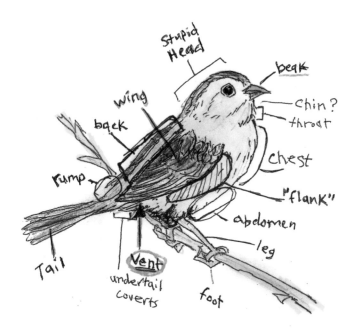

Short, fat, awkwardly tall, garishly colored, or poorly groomed, birds can look very different. But trust me, they all have pretty much the same parts. This sparrow is a good example: it is very boring, but it has the basic "bird" shape and all the standard bird options.

BIRD NEST IDENTIFICATION

If you're like me, when you come across a bird's nest, you will want to know what kind of idiot has made their home there. With some basic nest knowledge and an idea of what birds are common to the area, you can at least narrow it down to a few likely suspects.

MATERIALS: Is it constructed from straw, grasses, moss, leaves, hair (nasty), or twigs? You will need to learn which birds make their nests out of what materials, and what they might use instead if those materials are not conveniently available. Get ready for a lot of reading.

EGGS: Are they 14mm and blue with small brown spots? Or 12mm with brownish-red spots? Forget it. Unless you have a photographic memory and a lot of time on your hands, leave this one to the egg nerds.

SHAPE: Good news! There are only four shapes to memorize. This is something you can handle:

Cavity Nests

Basically just a hole where you can lay eggs. Usually pecked out by obsessive, destructive birds, but the lazier cavity nesters will simply find someone else's old hole and move in.

- Woodpeckers (destructive)
- Bluebirds (lazy)
- Wrens, etc. (mostly lazy)

Cup-Shaped Nests

This is the standard type of nest that you would think of. Most birds' nests fall into this category. They are made by birds who lack originality.

- American robins
- Barn swallows
- Warblers
- Tons of others, you name it

Pendant Nests

These dangling wrecks look like woven sacks of trash that hang from a branch or something. Built by messy birds.

- Baltimore orioles
- Most weaver birds
- Probably others

Platform Nests

These are flat structure with no sides. They typically belong to birds who either don't care about safety or completely lack any sense of proper nest design.

- Bald eagles
- Great blue herons
- Storks and other weirdos

REFERENCE

If you've ever witnessed the migration of birds and then wondered where do they all come from, and where do they go, then you should take a look at this map. Birds migrate along vast paths called "flyways."

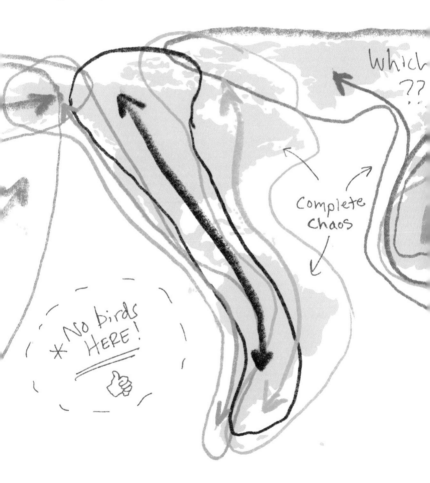

These flyways extend nearly pole to pole and overlap extensively in many places. Basically, birds just fly around this planet willy-nilly, like they think they own the fucking place.

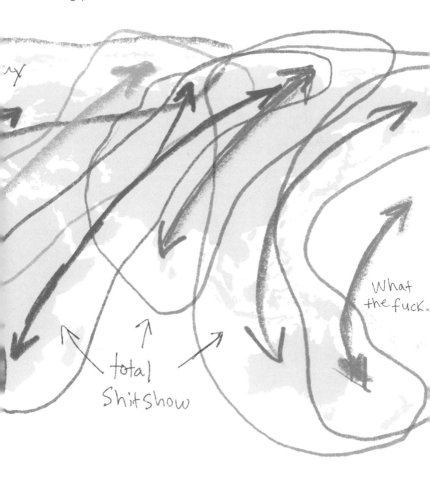

total Shitshow

What the fuck.

TIPS FOR JOURNALERS

OBSERVING FLOCKS

Most birds birds are generally small, so you are unlikely to become aware of an individual at long distance unless it is doing something flamboyantly stupid.

Large groups of birds are more obvious and therefore often spotted from much farther away. While you may not be able to observe the fine points of their behavior or markings at a distance, it may still be of some value to document what you can, such as location, time and weather, and their approximate numbers.

On the other hand, if you are journaling for personal enjoyment rather than ornithological study, it will suffice to make a quick note for your future reference. For instance, if you observed a large group of starlings you could just write "saw a whole bunch of ass-holes" and call it a day.

TIPS FOR JOURNALERS

KEEP A HANDFUL OF SEED IN YOUR POCKET

When wandering the forest paths with your eyes up and on the lookout for birds, you may occasionally run across another bird watcher. They may want to share information about which birds are in the vicinity, what you have both spotted, and where. Throwing a suprise handful of seed in their face can confuse and distract them, giving you valuable time to escape a potentially tedious conversation.

try Mixed Seed for best results.

Sunflower seeds are a good all-purpose deterrent.

not sure what these are, but they seem to work.

little bity ones cause a blinding cloud.

*NOTE: if the local birdwatchers are particularly friendly, you may wish to add UNSHELLED WALNUTS to your mix.

TIPS FOR JOURNALERS

HOW TO DRAW A BIRD

"How to draw a bird" is a question that I am frequently asked, although it is actually not a question or even a proper sentence. The important thing to remember is that in a personal field journal such as this, there is no need to be technically perfect or to capture every detail, unless you are some kind of artistic show-off. I mean, if you are such a genius with a pen, then why are you even reading this section? Whatever. Here are a few shortcuts, if you're not too talented to be bothered with them.

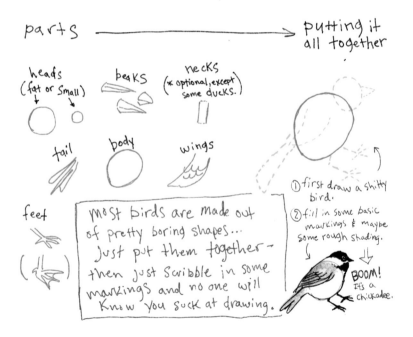

parts ⟶ putting it all together

heads (fat or small)

beaks

necks (* optional, except some ducks.)

tail

body

wings

feet

① first draw a shitty bird.

② fill in some basic markings & maybe some rough shading.

most birds are made out of pretty boring shapes... Just put them together - then just scribble in some markings and no one will know you suck at drawing.

BOOM! It's a chickadee.

Try drawing a bird
(any bird will do)

put that fat little twerp right here
↓

this general
vicinity

Remember:

- Start with
  a blob shape

- add another
  blob or two

- build on that
  by adding details

Or maybe just
freehand it —
who cares?

ABOUT THE AUTHOR

Matt Kracht was introduced to amateur ornithology in the fourth grade and has never gotten over the trauma. He lives in Tacoma, Washington, where he can be found wandering through the evergreens or along the beautiful waters of the Puget Sound and cursing at birds.

Follow him on Instagram **@mkracht**

MORE BIRD BOOKS BY THIS GUY

The Field Guide to Dumb Birds of North America

A humorous look at 50 common North American dumb birds. For those who have a disdain for birds or bird lovers with a sense of humor, this snarky, illustrated handbook is equal parts profane, funny, and—let's face it—true.

The Field Guide to Dumb Birds of the Whole Stupid World

Let's face it—all birds are jerks, no matter where in the world they reside. Following in the footsteps of *The Field Guide to Dumb Birds of North America*, this hilarious sequel ventures beyond to identify the stupidest birds around the world.